Ripley's AQUARIUM OF CANADA

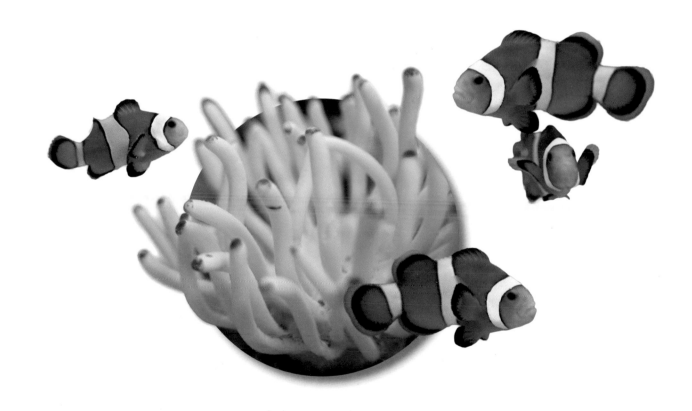

A COMMEMORATIVE GUIDE

Welcome to Ripley's Aquarium of Canada

We are proud to be a part of one of the greatest and most diverse metropolitan areas in the world. Right in the heart of downtown Toronto, we are located in front of the CN Tower and between the Rogers Centre and Metro Toronto Convention Centre. We are thrilled to call some pretty famous residents our neighbours—the Toronto Maple Leafs, Toronto Blue Jays, Toronto Argonauts and Toronto Raptors ensure that this area is always a bustling hub of activity. Like them, we aim to be an iconic landmark in this magnificent cityscape.

When we opened our doors in October of 2013, we made it our mission to establish a strong focus on education, conservation, and above all, entertainment.

From our range of school programs to each one of our interactive displays, the spotlight is always on education. Our goal is that the knowledge we share will foster lifelong relationships with the majestic oceans, lakes and rivers in our world.

Our zoological practices, research initiatives, and outreach schemes have conservation at their heart. We work hard to promote a culture of sustainability while building a legacy of ecological stewardship. Our husbandry team brings state-of-the-art care to our 16,000 aquatic animals and aims to meet the standards set by the Association of Zoos and Aquariums (AZA) and the Canadian Association of Zoos and Aquariums (CAZA). Ripley's also owns aquariums in Myrtle Beach, South Carolina, and Gatlinburg, Tennessee, and we are proud to say that they are both fully accredited by the AZA.

Above all, at Ripley's Aquarium of Canada we aim to entertain. Our diverse galleries aspire to stir wonder and amazement. We have traversed the globe to bring you the Waters of the World. From the indigenous Canadian Waters to our stunning Rainbow Reef, the details and exhibits in each gallery tell a better story than words ever could.

I hope you enjoy our showstopper, the Dangerous Lagoon. Longer than a football field, it features a glidepath that travels through the largest underwater tunnel in North America, taking you on a magical journey through an enormous 2.5-million-litre tank as sand tiger, sandbar and nurse sharks swim overhead.

I want to personally welcome you to Ripley's Aquarium of Canada. I hope you learn, take part in our conservation efforts, and most importantly, have fun!

Jim

Jim Pattison Jr.
President, Ripley Entertainment, Inc.

The Building Project

It takes vision, ambition and dedication to transform part of the urban landscape into an aquarium for 15,000 creatures within a range of complex habitats. It also takes time, money, exceptional architectural and engineering skills—and the combined efforts of a highly qualified, and committed, team of experts.

After three years of planning and design, construction of Ripley's Aquarium of Canada began in Toronto on July 20, 2011 and took a little over two years to complete. The result is an impressive downtown building that showcases a diverse and beautiful collection of some of the most fascinating aquatic creatures on the planet. The Aquarium also provides countless opportunities to educate and inspire all of us to protect the marine environment.

The early stages of construction included laying the huge pipes that carry an astonishing 5.7 million litres (1.5 million gallons) of water around the Aquarium's marine and freshwater habitats.

Upon completion, Ripley's Aquarium of Canada covered 12,500 square metres (135,000 square feet) in the heart of downtown Toronto.

The sheer scale of the building project could be seen from the top of the adjacent CN Tower.

Construction of the Aquarium's roof gets underway.

The roof's distinctive tile pattern begins to take shape.

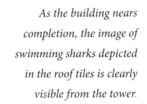

As the building nears completion, the image of swimming sharks depicted in the roof tiles is clearly visible from the tower.

The curved shape of the acrylic tunnel helps it to withstand the huge amount of pressure generated by the water in Dangerous Lagoon.

Part of the acrylic tunnel is lowered into place above the moving walkway that winds its way through Dangerous Lagoon—the stunning 2.84-million-litre (750,000-gallon) habitat that's home to the Aquarium's largest sharks.

Aquarium Husbandry

A large marine turtle is moved into an observation tank temporarily so its general health and wellbeing can be closely monitored.

Recreating the wild inside a city aquarium is a complex undertaking requiring skill and dedication. Behind the scenes, a team of highly experienced marine biologists, veterinarians and aquarists care for the 15,000 animals in residence. These experts are responsible for animal husbandry, and they also contribute to the Aquarium's conservation goals, scientific research and educational projects.

Checking the water's chemistry is an essential task. The husbandry staff work with the Operations Department to ensure the life-support systems and filtration processes are all working well.

The husbandry team is kept very busy. Caring for the animals includes routine jobs, such as feeding and testing the water, but it also requires a high level of knowledge of each species. The team is always on the look out for unusual behaviour, or any signs of illness. They also ensure each animal has an enriching environment, allowing it to behave much as it would in its natural environment.

A member of the husbandry team hand feeds the inhabitants of the pufferfish exhibit.

Animal nutrition is a complicated science, and the husbandry team works hard to imitate an animal's natural diet. Animals are mostly fed with restaurant-quality seafood that may be supplemented with plants, such as bok choy, for the vegetarians. The quantity and type of food varies daily, just as it would in the wild.

The animal husbandry team includes nine staff divers who help to look after the collection. Feeding animals inside a tank is a highly specialized job. All the tanks are cleaned daily, but large tanks are typically scrubbed by scuba divers, usually before or after visitor opening hours.

IT'S A FACT
Animal husbandry (caring for animals) is a human skill that dates back at least to Neolithic times—10,000 years ago.

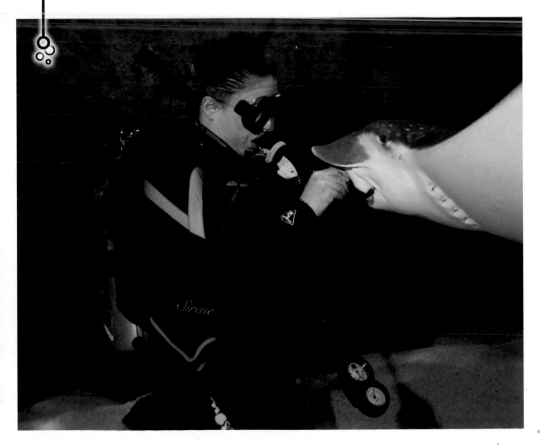

From feeding the animals to caring for the habitats in which they live, every member of the Aquarium husbandry team is committed to maintaining the highest standards of animal welfare, and to inspiring and educating visitors in matters of marine conservation.

Our Top Ten

There are so many incredible creatures in Ripley's Aquarium of Canada that it has been really difficult to choose our top ten, but here they are. We proudly present some of our very favourite exhibits, and give you a little information about why they are so special.

Big, brainy and biologically fascinating, our giant Pacific octopus has it all. With a maximum armspan of 5 metres (16 feet) this is the largest species of octopus and one of the world's largest invertebrates.

Sawfish are rays with shark-like bodies that grow to 4 metres (13 feet) or more. Their long, toothed snouts (saws) are formidable weapons that are used to swipe at passing shoals of fish.

Green sea turtles cross entire oceans on annual migrations of 2,000 kilometres (1,200 miles) or more. They swim from their foraging to breeding grounds using navigational skills that are still little understood.

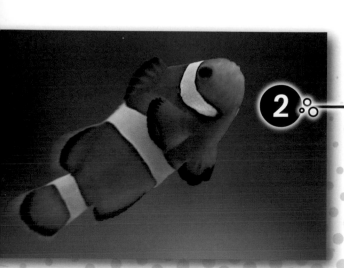

The most iconic of coral fish, the stunning clownfish is famous as the star of Disney's Finding Nemo. This is the only fish known to live amid the stinging tentacles of anemones.

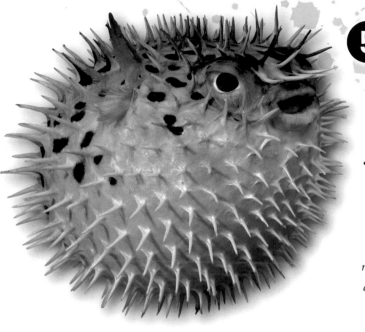

5

Many animals make themselves look bigger when under attack, but pufferfish are masters of this deceptive art. By gulping water, they can swell into a spiky ball several times their natural size.

6

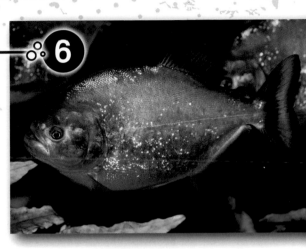

This ferocious-looking fish enjoys a reputation as a ruthless killer. Red-bellied piranhas are equipped with razor sharp teeth that deliver an effective and forceful bite, but these fish prey mostly on small river creatures.

7

Unlike other sharks, sand tigers have an unusual habit of gulping air from the ocean's surface. The swallowed air aids their buoyancy and allows them to float motionless, waiting for prey.

8

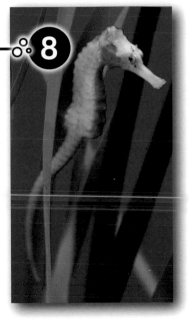

Seahorses are among the most extraordinary of all fish, with their small upright bodies and poor swimming abilities. Even stranger, it is seahorse fathers, not mothers, that give birth to the tiny fry.

9

Some jellies are also known as sea nettles because of their stinging tentacles. The largest jellies have tentacles many metres long, but it's the tiny box jellyfish that is one of the most venomous.

An almost invisible inhabitant of the seabed, a camouflaged southern stingray protects itself with venomous spines at the base of its long slender tail. The venom can be deadly to other animals, and causes great pain for humans.

10

With every drop of water you drink,

every breath you take,

you're connected to the sea.

No matter where on Earth you live.

~

SYLVIA EARLE

Canadian Waters

Canada is famous all over the world for its breathtaking landscapes and their resident wildlife, but its waters are an even greater treasure trove of extraordinary habitats and animals.

As you explore the Canadian Waters gallery you will journey from coast to coast via freshwater wildernesses, fisheries and kelp forests. Take in the impressive biodiversity of the Great Lakes—they account for 20 per cent of the world's fresh water and are an essential part of Canada's freshwater habitat. And with three oceans to choose from, it's no wonder our marine habitats are home to such a variety of flora and fauna.

American lobsters are crustaceans, and closely related to crabs. They live on rocky shores but are sensitive to water temperature. As the world's seas warm up, these coldwater lobsters must move northwards to cooler habitats.

Eels are long-bodied fish that typically have about 100 vertebrae in their highly flexible spines. American eels inhabit fresh water, but undergo intriguing migrations of over 3,000 kilometres (1,875 miles) to spawn in the Atlantic Ocean's Sargasso Sea.

Canadian cod were close to extinction in the early 1990s, but their populations are now slowly growing, thanks to conservation efforts. Cod feed on small, plankton-eating fish and may grow to a length of 2 metres (6.5 feet), and reach 25 years of age.

The Great Lakes exhibit features lake sturgeons, which can grow to 2 metres (6.5 feet), making them North America's largest freshwater fish. Once common, before heavy fishing took its toll, these "living fossils" can survive for 150 years.

The alewife's original home was the Atlantic Coast, although this small herring is now well established in the Great Lakes. A shoaling fish, it is particularly sensitive to environmental changes in its freshwater habitat.

Giant Pacific octopuses are large and extremely clever molluscs that can grow up to 15 kilos (33 pounds) in weight, with an arm span of up to 4.3 metres (14 feet). They can change their skin colour and even its texture to blend into their environment.

Lumpfish are found mostly on or near the seabed in the northern Atlantic Ocean, to depths of up to 1,000 metres (3,300 feet). They have partially joined pelvic fins that form a suction cup, which helps them to hold on to rocks in the turbulent sea.

Tube anemones are unusual creatures related to sea anemones. They have two whorls of stinging tentacles encircling the mouth and can withdraw into their tube, which is usually partially buried in the seabed.

Alaskan king crabs can grow to be huge, with a leg span of up to 1.8 metres (6 feet). There are several species of king crab in Alaska, and they are probably best known for being caught in large quantities for the table.

Wolf eels have long, snake-like bodies, but are not true eels. They have strong heads and jaws, and sharp teeth—an excellent combination for eating crustaceans and spiny sea urchins. Wolf eels grow to more than 2 metres (6½ feet) long.

IT'S A FACT

Octopuses in aquariums have been known to use their ingenuity to sneak out of their tanks at night and feast on fish in nearby exhibits.

Kelp Forest

A trip through the Kelp Forest exhibit is a journey through an underwater jungle. A constant wave swell sways the giant kelp fronds, while rockfish dart through the beams of light. Like tropical rainforests, kelp habitats are unique environments. They support complex ecosystems, providing a refuge for young organisms and grazing grounds for shellfish.

"Kelp" was once the name for ashes from burned seaweed that were used to make soap and glass. Today, it applies to all large brown seaweeds, which are not typical plants because they lack stems, roots and leaves. Kelp forms huge, dense undersea forests in rocky lower shore and intertidal zones. It dampens wave energy, reducing coastal erosion and creating a sheltered habitat. Giant kelp can grow to 30 metres (100 feet) high. Fast-growing kelp produces slime on its fronds, which prevents animals settling on it. As the rate of growth slows, the slime production decreases and small creatures such as tube-worms can grow on the kelp. The kelp then sheds old fronds to get rid of these unwelcome squatters.

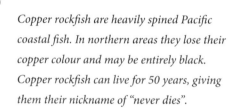

Copper rockfish are heavily spined Pacific coastal fish. In northern areas they lose their copper colour and may be entirely black. Copper rockfish can live for 50 years, giving them their nickname of "never dies".

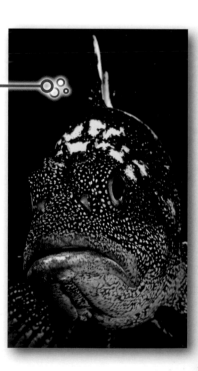

China rockfish have stout bodies and strong head spines. These fish are solitary animals and very territorial. They rarely move more than 10 metres (30 feet) away from their home site.

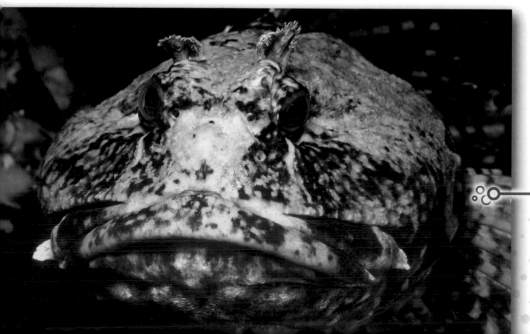

Cabezons live close to the sea floor. Greeny-brown mottled colouring, algae-like head growths and a stocky body help cabezons to lurk, unseen, on the rocky seabed of a kelp forest.

Kelp grows best in *cold, shallow water and can grow at a rate of 1 metre (3 feet) a day. Its fronds usually contain gas-filled bubbles that keep it buoyant, allowing the seaweed to extend towards the sunlight that it needs to photosynthesize.*

Rainbow Reef

Watching fish dart around a reef is strangely satisfying. While colour and movement captivate the senses, the calm serenity of light-filtering water can bewitch any Aquarium visitor.

The Rainbow Reef beautifully recreates the warm and inviting coral seas of the Indo-Pacific Ocean. Here you can enjoy the kaleidoscope of fish that dart around their idyllic home, and learn more about their precious but endangered habitats. In the wild, reef-building coral animals are extraordinary architects, but they are fussy about the cleanliness, temperature, salinity and clarity of seawater. As our oceans warm and suffer pollution, coral reefs around the world are dying.

Triggerfish are beautiful, but notoriously bad-tempered and territorial. These specimens are clown triggerfish, and their natural habitat is the coral reefs of the Indo-Pacific.

Flourishing butterflyfish populations indicate that a reef is thriving. Raccoon butterflyfish inhabit coral reefs of the tropical Indo-Pacific Ocean. They are normally seen in pairs, or small groups.

Many coral reef fish risk bold colours and patterns rather than camouflage. There are always plenty of hiding places around a reef that these fish can dart into, and their colours might warn predators of spines or venom.

The unicorn fish is a plant-eating member of the surgeonfish group. Unicorn fish have a strange horn on their head, but when they fight they use spines on their tail, not their horns.

Damselfish are small coral fish and inhabit shallow zones in a coral reef. They can be territorial and males undertake complex courtship rituals to impress potential partners.

Schooling fish, such as these bluestripe snapper, are common around reefs. They enjoy some safety in numbers by confusing predators with their sudden co-ordinated movements and flashy colours or silvery scales.

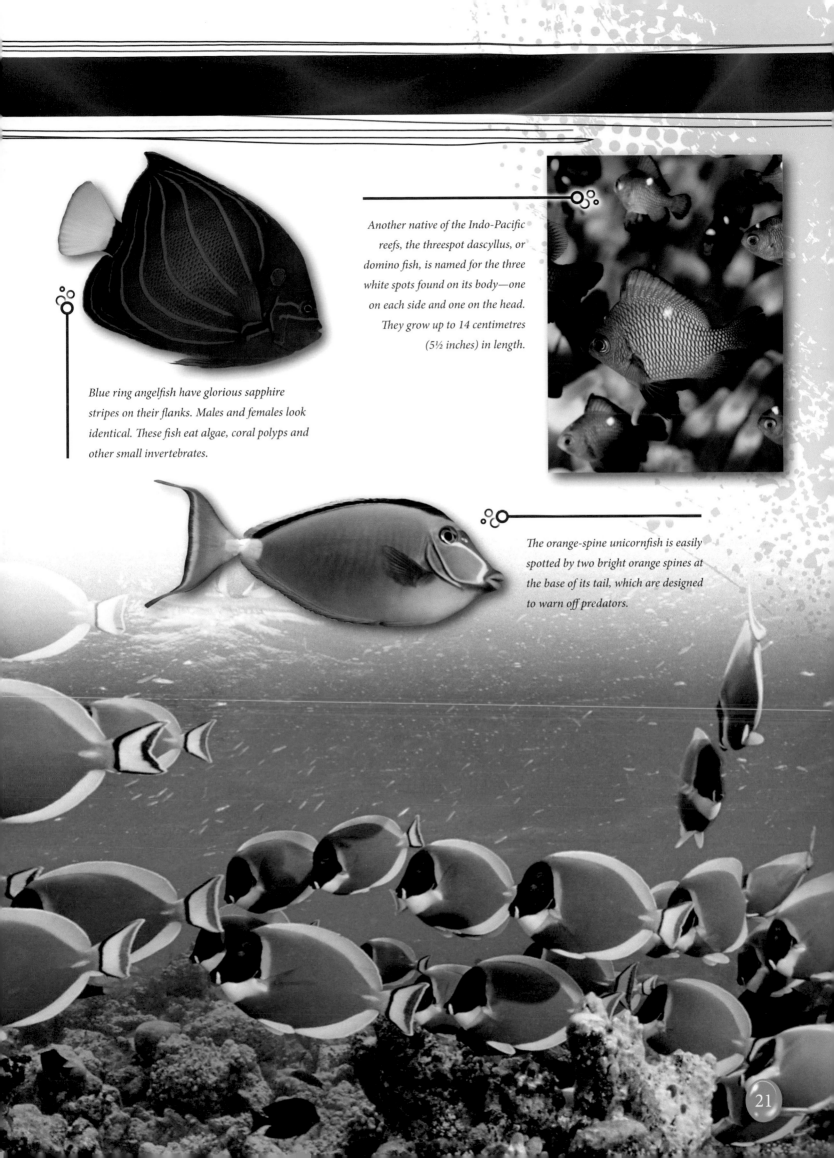

Blue ring angelfish have glorious sapphire stripes on their flanks. Males and females look identical. These fish eat algae, coral polyps and other small invertebrates.

Another native of the Indo-Pacific reefs, the threespot dascyllus, or domino fish, is named for the three white spots found on its body—one on each side and one on the head. They grow up to 14 centimetres (5½ inches) in length.

The orange-spine unicornfish is easily spotted by two bright orange spines at the base of its tail, which are designed to warn off predators.

Look deep into nature, and then you will understand everything better.

~

ALBERT EINSTEIN

Smaller Sharks

Coral reefs cover less than one per cent of the world's oceans, yet they provide a habitat for a quarter of all marine species. It's no wonder that predators such as smaller sharks prowl around reefs in search of rich pickings—they are almost spoiled for choice.

Reef sharks feed mostly on reef fish, cephalopods (squid, octopus and cuttlefish), lobsters, crabs and shrimp. In general, they give birth to live young that take about five years to reach maturity. Many species of reef shark have suffered drops in their populations, including blacktips and zebra sharks. Conservation work to limit human fishing for sharks, and to protect coral reefs, may help to reverse the recent decline in reef shark numbers.

Blacktips are not fussy eaters and can cope with a wide range of prey, including toxic, spined porcupinefish and stingrays. In turn, they are preyed upon by humans, especially around the Indian Ocean and South China Sea.

Zebra sharks, also known as leopard sharks, have greyish brown bodies with bold spotted markings. They are sluggish swimmers that often rest on the seabed, with their mouth open. Adults grow to 3.5 metres (11½ feet) and have a long thresher-like tail to help propel them through the ocean.

Finding an ornate wobbegong is a challenge—you may not know one is there even if you are staring it in the face! These fish are among the most impressive of animals, with phenomenal camouflage and body shapes that combine to create an "invisibility cloak". They simply blend into their environment and disappear.

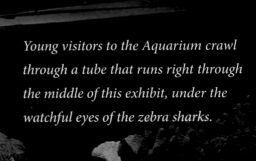

Young visitors to the Aquarium crawl through a tube that runs right through the middle of this exhibit, under the watchful eyes of the zebra sharks.

Dangerous Lagoon

A dive through the Dangerous Lagoon will introduce you to some of the Aquarium's most fearsome-looking creatures. Protected from specimens of three species of shark inside the 96-metre-long (315-feet) tunnel, you will be able to get up close and personal with some of the ocean's most awesome creatures.

Travelling along the moving walkway within this enormous exhibit allows observers a unique viewpoint. Sharks can be observed from underneath—the perfect way to see the jagged teeth of a sand tiger shark. Once you've seen this predator's mouth you will understand why it's also known as the "ragged-tooth". Look out for the myriad other animals that share this special ecosystem, including sawfish, rays, moray eels and green sea turtles.

Sand tiger sharks can grow to 3 metres (10 feet) or more. They thrive in aquariums, giving observers the chance to see a predatory shark up close.

Considered to be one of the most beautiful fish in the world, the queen angelfish is both iridescent and resplendent. The crown-like mark on the forehead gives this fish its royal name.

IT'S A FACT

Visitors can walk beneath Dangerous Lagoon and gaze up at its inhabitants through clear acrylic panels that are 80 milliimetres (3 inches) thick.

Sandbars are among the largest of coastal sharks. Like other sharks, they detect their prey by sensing the tiny electrical fields produced by another animal's body.

Named after its military-like stripes, the sergeant major is common in warm waters, especially around reefs. The males build nests for the eggs, and guard up to 200,000 of them at a time.

The roughtail stingray is one of the largest stingrays in the Atlantic Ocean. It dives deep in search of crabs, fish, molluscs and shrimps. Stingrays are often hard to see because they lie on the seabed under a dusting of sand or mud.

Porkfish live in large schools and are most active at night. They belong to a group of fish called grunts, so named because they grind their teeth together and make a grunting sound.

Visitors to the Aquarium can crawl into a pop-up submersible in the Discovery Centre, which takes them right into the heart of Dangerous Lagoon for an unbeatable close-up look at its inhabitants.

Green sea turtles are one of seven species of marine turtle, all of which are classified as endangered, or critically endangered. This is largely due to pollution, fishing and loss of their habitats. The Aquarium supports a number of conservation initiatives to raise awareness and help protect these magnificent sea creatures.

If you encounter a giant grouper while underwater take careful note of its body language—a shaking body, open mouth and deep rumbling signify that this huge fish is not happy. Attacks by groupers can be dangerous, not least because they can reach a massive 3 metres (10 feet) in length.

Squirrelfish typically grow to between 15 and 35 centimetres (6 and 14 inches) in length. They have unusually large eyes, which help these nocturnal creatures to see better at night.

Green moray eels are solitary creatures that hide in rocky crevices during the day, emerging at night to hunt. Powerful predators growing up to 2.5 metres (8 feet) long, they are actually a blue-grey colour but are covered in a layer of yellow mucus that protects them from parasites and gives them their green tint.

IT'S A FACT
Moray eels have long, smooth and slimy bodies and sharp dog-like teeth. They are one of the few species of fish that can swim backwards.

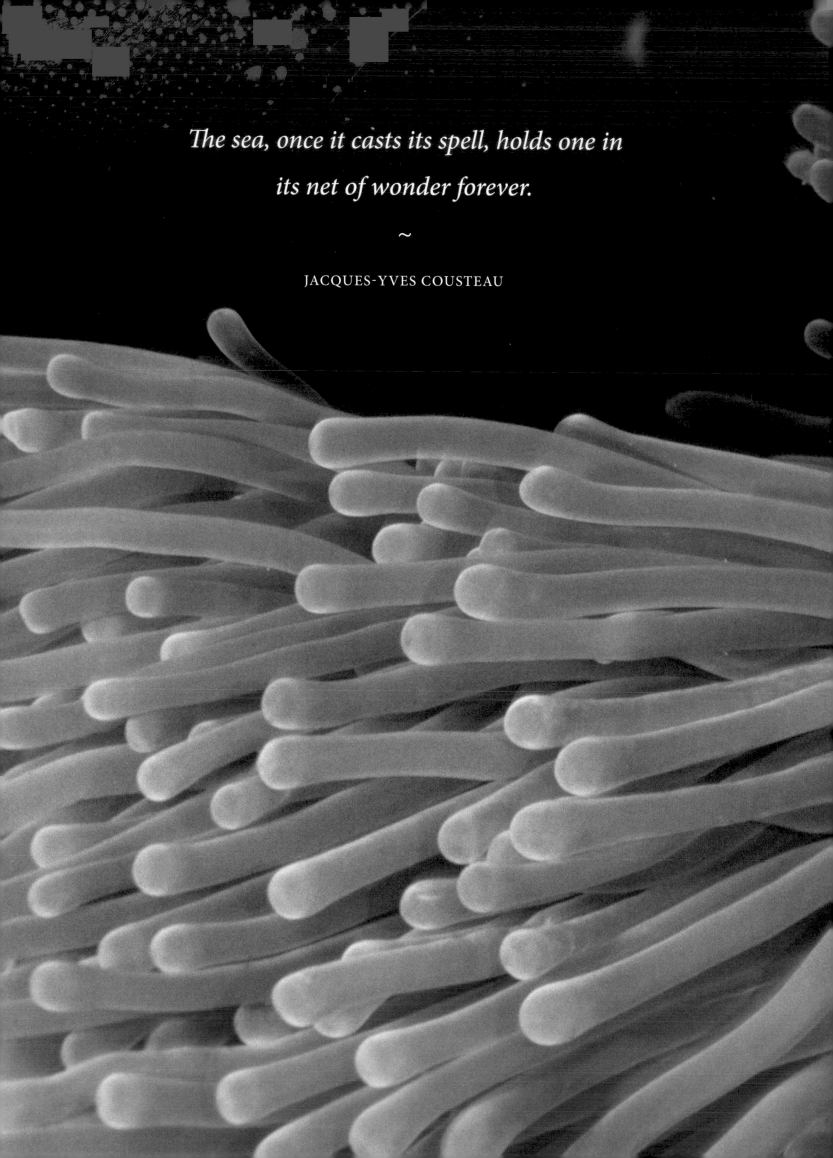

The sea, once it casts its spell, holds one in
its net of wonder forever.

~

JACQUES-YVES COUSTEAU

Discovery Centre

Bringing the underwater world to life by providing wonderful opportunities to watch and engage with a thriving ecosystem is a challenge for all aquariums. Here at the Discovery Centre we believe we've combined technology with nature to achieve that aim.

Clownfish enjoy an extraordinary relationship with sea anemones. Protected from an anemone's stinging tentacles by a layer of mucus, these fish swim among anemones to keep safe from predators.

The pop-up viewing bubbles allow observers to get an intimate look at deadly fish—such as porcupinefish and puffers—without harm to either human or animal. Enjoy the sensation of a deep-sea dive in an interactive submarine without having to worry about getting wet. You can also interact with some fascinating ancient marine wildlife "hands on" at the large horseshoe crab touch pool.

The clownfish pop-up tank gives visitors a unique chance to be surrounded by these beautiful creatures.

Palette surgeonfish are named after a black "artist's palette-shaped" marking on their sides. They are usually seen swimming in pairs, or small groups.

The Discovery Centre is a favourite place for visitors to find out more about the dynamics of the marine environment through play. Young visitors can have fun with a water table that replicates the complex lock system of the Great Lakes.

With their stunning mauve and yellow bodies, it is not surprising that royal grammas are popular with aquarium enthusiasts. They are often forced to hide in cracks and crevices, however, as they are popular prey for bigger fish.

During the day, yellow tangs are a solid, golden yellow colour. At night, a brown patch and horizontal white line on each side become more visible.

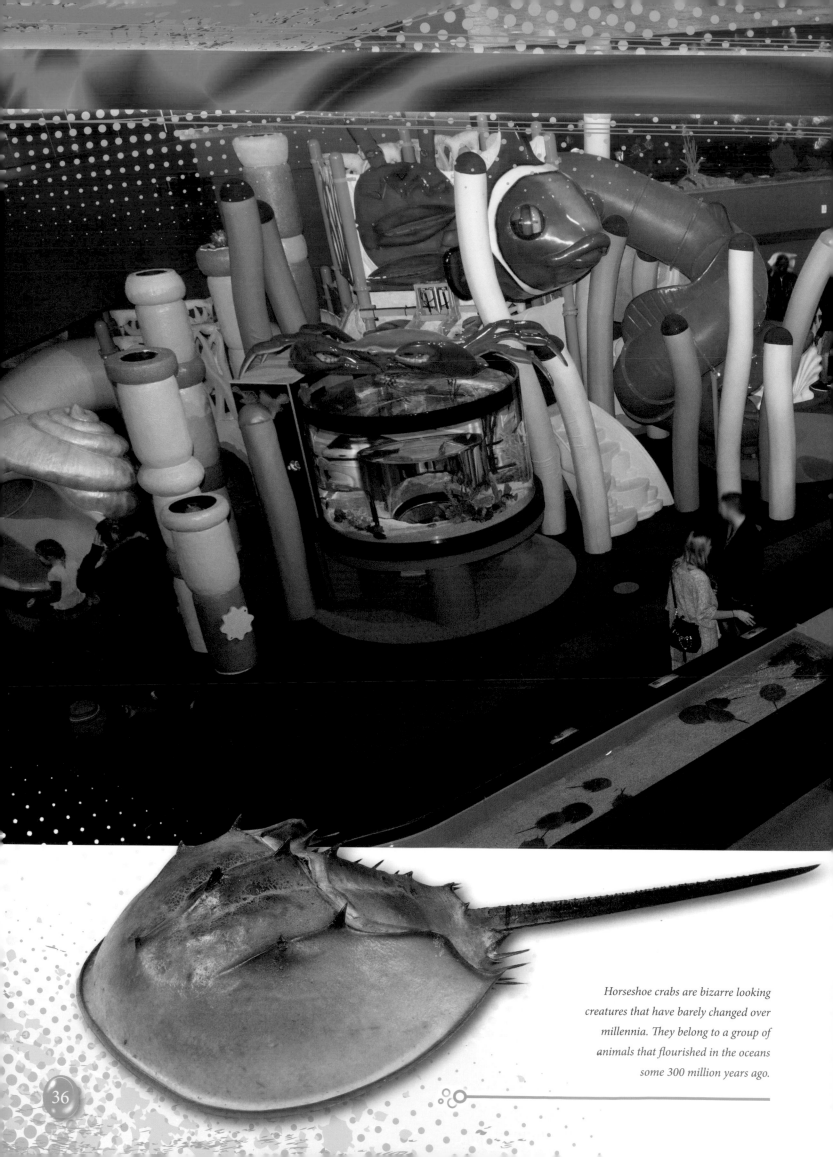

Horseshoe crabs are bizarre looking creatures that have barely changed over millennia. They belong to a group of animals that flourished in the oceans some 300 million years ago.

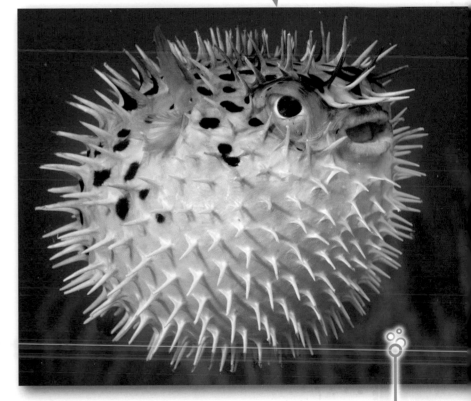

Pufferfish (seen deflated, left), live mostly around reefs, mangroves and seagrass beds. They can grow up to 35 centimetres (14 inches) in length.

The Discovery Centre is packed with interactive exhibits for all the family to enjoy.

A pufferfish inflates its body by taking in water when it feels threatened. In this mode its spines stand erect, and its skin colour may change.

Ripley's aquarists are on hand to show visitors how they can interact with horseshoe crabs in the horseshoe crab touch pool. These strange ancient creatures are slow-moving and harmless and, despite their name, are more closely related to spiders than crabs.

IT'S A FACT
Pufferfish are known as "fugu" in Japan where they are a delicacy, even though parts of a pufferfish's body contain a poison that's 1,200 times more lethal than cyanide.

The Gallery

The living things within an ecosystem rely on the maintenance of a fragile balance. When you experience The Gallery you will not only find stunning fish in technicolour hues, you will be witnessing the incredible adaptations employed in historic battles for survival.

The story of most ecosystems is wrapped up in predator-prey relationships. Evolutionary advantages that help a predator to feed, and reproduce, will be carried onto the next generation. These adaptations are just as necessary for prey. That is why the huge variety of animals in The Gallery are testament to the ways animals have adapted, and continue to adapt, in a continuous fight for life.

The spellbinding creatures in The Gallery display a range of fascinating characteristics that they have evolved to survive. The mighty lionfish has few natural predators because of its highly effective venomous spines.

Sailfin tangs help maintain the health of a coral reef. They graze on the tiny algae that grow on a reef, and this allows the sunlight to reach the reef-building polyps that need light to survive.

It takes a keen eye to find a leafy seadragon—they are master mimics of seaweed. Seadragons and seahorses are poor swimmers—their survival lies in an ability to "disappear" into their environment.

Native to South America, the red-bellied
piranha travels in shoals as a defence against
larger predators. Although they do not
co-ordinate their attacks, these fish are famous
for their carnivorous feeding frenzies.

Most predators ambush, chase or trap their prey. Archerfish are far more sophisticated than that. They live mostly in rivers, and catch airborne or resting insects by shooting them down with a jet of water from their mouths. The powerful spray of water is achieved when the fish presses its tongue against a groove in its mouth, to create a "gun-barrel" shape. The jet is accurate to a distance of 2 metres (6½ feet), and can knock an insect from an overhanging leaf into the water.

The reef stonefish is probably the most venomous fish in the world, and one of the most deadly. Its highly camouflaged body enables this seabed dweller to blend into a rocky sea floor.

Cuttlefish, such as this European cuttlefish, are closely related to squid and octopuses and have eight arms and two long tentacles. Cuttlefish are able to change colour at will—an extraordinary adaptation that continues to challenge scientists' understanding of evolution.

Not all fish live in water. Atlantic mud-skippers are amphibious—which means they are able to live at sea, but also on land, where they breathe air and use their pectoral fins to crawl about.

Sometimes called "rainforests of the sea", coral reefs are rich in life, with a variety of organisms that is rarely equalled. The structure of a reef lends itself to creating not just one habitat, but thousands of micro-habitats. Animals have evolved to survive in these micro-habitats, and often exhibit extraordinary adaptations and specialist lifestyles. When a reef dies—which is sometimes a purely natural phenomenon, but is increasingly the result of man's careless treatment of the environment— highly-adapted species are likely to become extinct.

The slender spines of a lionfish are like hypodermic needles, and can inject venom deep into the flesh of another animal, or human.

A longsnout sea horse uses its flexible tail to anchor itself to sea grasses, corals and mangroves. It catches and kills its main prey— shrimp and other small crustaceans— pusing its long snout.

The long, slender snout of the copperband butterflyfish is the ideal shape for poking into small spaces and feeding on small invertebrates.

Ray Bay

Rays have flat bodies and are mostly placid, graceful fish that are visually very different to their cousins, the sharks. Like sharks and skates, rays do not have bony skeletons, but ones made of flexible cartilage instead.

Female rays keep their fertilized eggs inside their bodies while they develop. This strategy means they can give birth to live young, having protected their eggs from predation. Here at Ray Bay you can see how some rays use their flattened bodies and large, modified pectoral fins like wings to "fly" through the water. Notice the shape and position of a ray's mouth—perfect for scooping up and crunching on hard-shelled animals on the ocean floor.

If you are lucky enough to get a close look at the underside of a ray, you may notice that its lower jaw is only loosely connected to its skull. This is so that the jaw can extend towards prey and create a suction force.

Come and touch these amazing creatures and learn more about them from our expert Aquarium guides.

A southern stingray can reach a body width of 2 metres (6½ feet). These flat fish feed on the seabed, but protect themselves with a spine on their tail, which has between 52 and 80 "teeth" on each side.

Cownose rays, which can grow to over 1 metre (3 feet) in width, undertake long migrations in groups, travelling across the Atlantic Ocean. It is thought that they use water temperature and the orientation of the sun to help guide them.

IT'S A FACT
The world's largest ray is the manta ray. Despite reaching a huge 9 metres (30 feet) in width, these marine monsters feed mostly on plankton and small fish. They are harmless to humans.

Spotted eagle rays are common in coral reefs and, occasionally, in estuaries. They usually swim in groups and can be seen leaping fully out of the water.

Rays move with incredible grace. The Aquarium's large observation windows offer the perfect opportunity for children to experience the thrill of watching nature at close quarters.

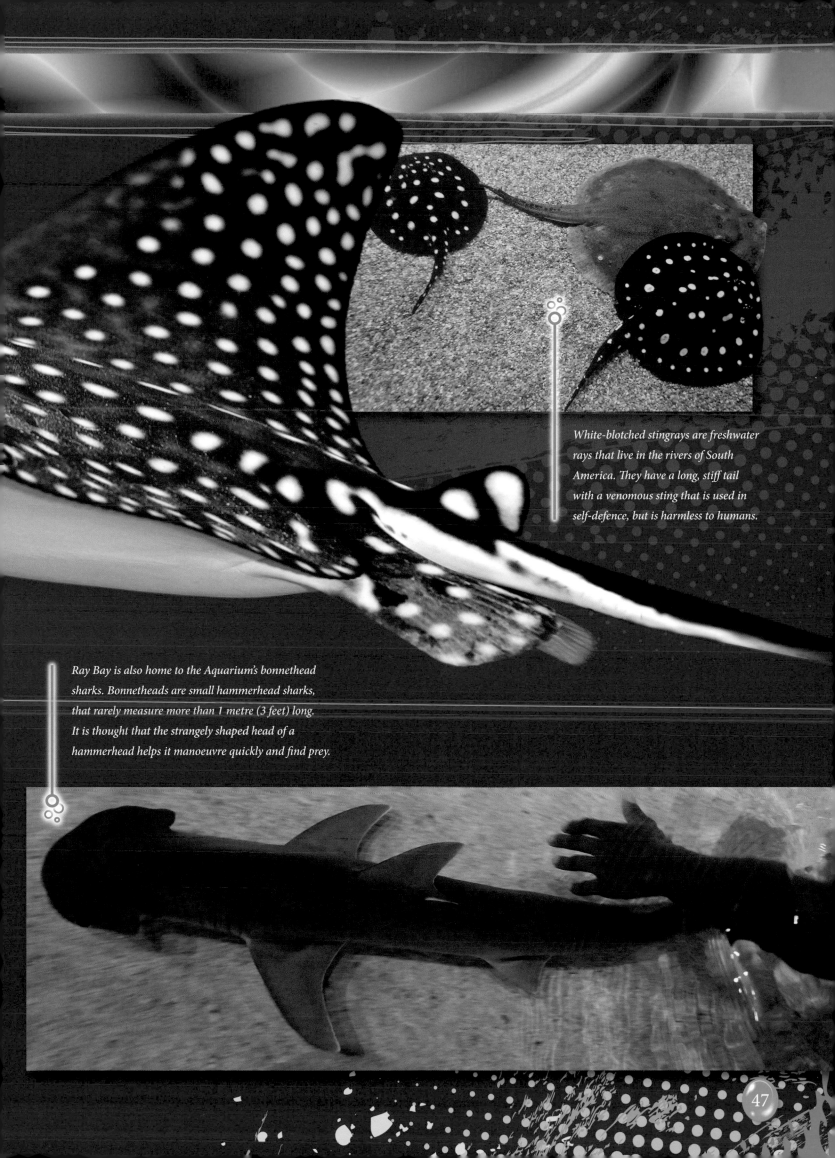

White-blotched stingrays are freshwater rays that live in the rivers of South America. They have a long, stiff tail with a venomous sting that is used in self-defence, but is harmless to humans.

Ray Bay is also home to the Aquarium's bonnethead sharks. Bonnetheads are small hammerhead sharks, that rarely measure more than 1 metre (3 feet) long. It is thought that the strangely shaped head of a hammerhead helps it manoeuvre quickly and find prey.

Shoreline Gallery

In the Touch and Learn area of the Shoreline Gallery you get to do more than just watch animals; you have the opportunity to practise real science. You can closely observe and touch the species on display, and see how their body shape and structure gives clues about their lifestyles.

Fish biologists have to make observations about animals without always having the luxury of getting as close to their specimens as you can here. Moving slowly, and quietly, will keep the animals relaxed as you approach them and offer the best opportunity to study their bodies, observe their behaviour—and gently touch their skin.

Shark skin is covered with tooth-like scales called dermal denticles. They are covered in enamel, just like our teeth, and give a shark's skin a surprisingly rough touch.

If you look closely at the head of a whitespotted bamboo shark you will notice a hole below each eye. These are spiracles, and they allow bottom-living sharks and rays to draw in water for breathing.

Epaulette sharks live in coastal waters around northern Australia and New Guinea. They can survive being caught in tide pools or exposed reef flats by shutting down some of their body functions for a few hours.

Come and experience close contact with some incredible wildlife in the Shoreline Gallery. Peer down into beautiful Ray Bay after interacting with these friendly creatures and their small shark cousins.

The world's finest wilderness

lies beneath the waves.

~

WYLAND

Planet Jellies

Ocean explorers sometimes encounter creatures that simply don't appear to belong on this planet. We continually learn about ocean wildlife, yet extraordinary appearances, outlandish life cycles and bizarre behaviour still strike us as "alien".

Jellies epitomize this "alien" phenomenon. They look like umbrellas, can be bigger than a human, or smaller than a tack, and have stinging tentacles. Yet they are poor swimmers and are subject to the whims of ocean currents. Travel to our Planet Jellies gallery—one of the largest of its kind in the world—and learn more about four species of jellies, beautifully exhibited in backlit tanks and colour-changing displays. Watch the mesmerizing sea nettles moving around their enormous kreisel tank, which has a gentle circular water flow designed to keep these delicate creatures safe in the aquarium environment.

IT'S A FACT
Jellyfish tentacles are lined with tiny stinging cells that can fire a harpoon-like barb and inject venom.

Pacific sea nettles lack eyes, but they have light-sensing organs that they use to undertake a daily migration from deep water to the sunlit surface water above.

Huge swarms of sea nettles have become more common in recent times, possibly because their natural predators (fish and sea turtles) are falling in number.

Moon jellies feed on tiny animals—
zooplankton—that get stuck on their
sticky mucus-covered body. Tiny hairs
called cilia move the food into canals that
lead towards the animal's stomach.

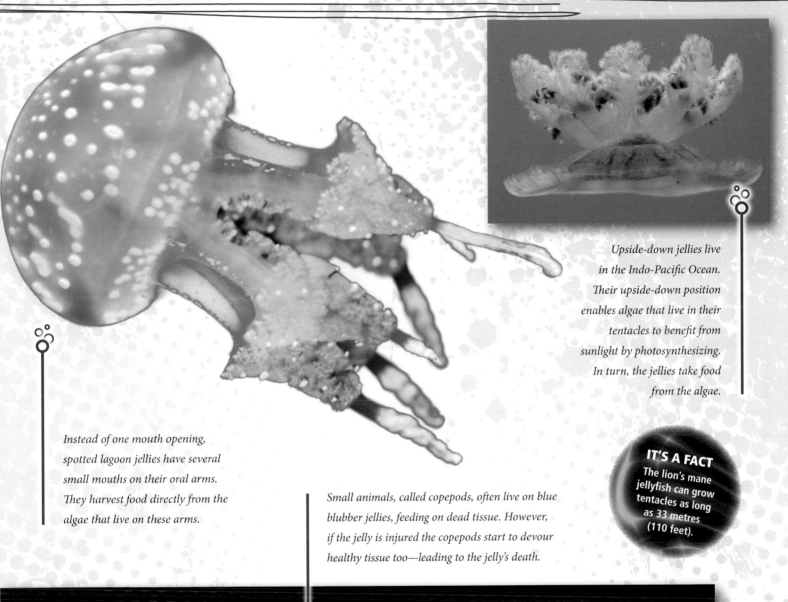

Upside-down jellies live in the Indo-Pacific Ocean. Their upside-down position enables algae that live in their tentacles to benefit from sunlight by photosynthesizing. In turn, the jellies take food from the algae.

Instead of one mouth opening, spotted lagoon jellies have several small mouths on their oral arms. They harvest food directly from the algae that live on these arms.

Small animals, called copepods, often live on blue blubber jellies, feeding on dead tissue. However, if the jelly is injured the copepods start to devour healthy tissue too—leading to the jelly's death.

IT'S A FACT
The lion's mane jellyfish can grow tentacles as long as 33 metres (110 feet).

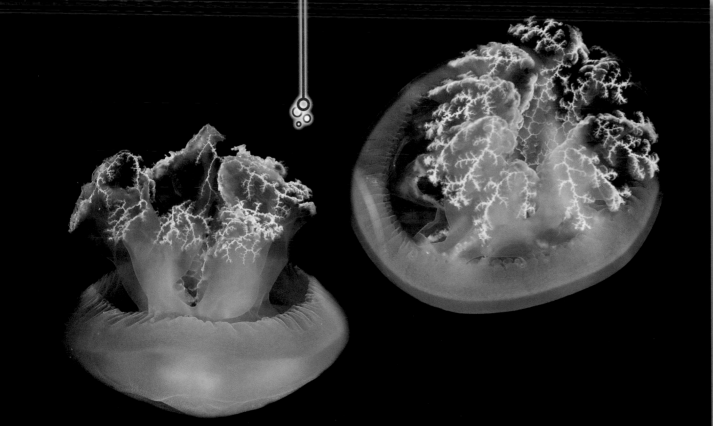

How It Works

Here at the Aquarium we like to believe we are masters of illusion. Our aim is to provide both our animals and our guests with a realistic marine experience but, like all great illusions, there is a great deal of work going on behind the scenes.

Explore the magic behind your aquatic experience in the Life Support System gallery. By bringing a significant amount of pumping and filtration equipment out into the public areas, the Aquarium offers visitors a unique opportunity to see how its complex environment is maintained.

Scrolling LED screens give visitors real-time updates on the conditions in the largest of the tanks.

Ninety-eight per cent of the Aquarium's water is treated for reuse, which means there is a constant recycling of almost all of the water in the building.

The Aquarium uses an incredible 2.84 million litres (750,000 gallons) of Toronto municipal water and runs it through carbon filters to remove any impurities. After this process is complete, the water is either circulated throughout the building for the Aquarium's freshwater systems or used as a base to make saltwater for the marine exhibits. The saltwater is custom-made using a recipe designed to mimic seawater. All of the components used are of a food grade quality and comprise major, minor and trace elements.

Young visitors enjoy playing with an interactive exhibit in the gallery. By moving plastic balls through a series of pipes and tanks they can learn about some of the steps taken by the Aquarium to ensure healthy water for all of its inhabitants.

Conserve Educate Inspire!

Ripley's Aquarium of Canada offers a truly unforgettable learning experience for children and adults alike. Our mission is to provide top quality, world-class aquatic life facilities that foster environmental education, conservation and research, while at the same time providing outstanding entertainment for visitors of all ages.

Water covers 70 per cent of the Earth and is home to 94 per cent of all life on our planet. Almost all of the water on Earth is in the sea, yet we have explored less than 5 per cent of this vast realm. The oceans shape our climate and weather but we know more about the surface of the Moon than the ocean floor. The ocean is the heart of our planet's life-support system and here at the Aquarium, we believe it is our duty to learn about it and protect it.

A powerful advocate for environmental conservation at every level, the Aquarium wants to offer everyone the opportunity to get involved in conservation. It organizes beach sweeps and river rummages so we can improve our communities, and raise awareness of environmental issues.

The Aquarium encourages everyone, whatever their age, to take an active role in looking after our rivers and oceans, and by doing so to inspire others to do the same.

The Aquarium provides a diverse and exciting range of educational programs. They have been designed to meet provincial and state curriculum standards, but—more importantly—their aim is to inspire participants to protect and conserve our oceans.

Did you know that jellies...

- Live in the sea and are found in all oceans
- Have been on Earth for millions of years, and were around before the dinosaurs
- Can be very hard to see, and are sometimes almost invisible to the human eye
- Are not actually fish, despite commonly being called "jellyfish"
- Can travel in groups of over 100,000
- Have no brain but some species have eyes
- Use their tentacles to sting— most of their stings are harmless to humans but stings from some species, such as the box jelly, can be very painful and can even sometimes kill
- Can be bigger than a human or as small as a pinhead
- Are mainly made up of water and protein
- Are the favourite meal of many sea turtles

Custodians of the Planet

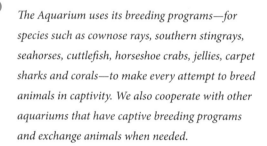

Here at the Aquarium we are passionate about our mission to inspire marine stewards of all generations. One key way we do this is by developing and supporting strategies to promote environmental awareness and sustainability.

Through our research initiatives, educational programs and outreach events—such as participation in the Great Canadian Shoreline Cleanup campaign—we aim to engage as many people as possible to take a role in protecting the world in which we live.

The Aquarium uses its breeding programs—for species such as cownose rays, southern stingrays, seahorses, cuttlefish, horseshoe crabs, jellies, carpet sharks and corals—to make every attempt to breed animals in captivity. We also cooperate with other aquariums that have captive breeding programs and exchange animals when needed.

Marine litter is a growing problem around the world. It has a profound impact on ocean wildlife. That's why staff are committed to not using plastic bottles at the Aquarium. However, the Aquarium believes that each one of us has an impact on the planet and we can all take responsibility for a few simple changes in our daily lives that can influence its future. Follow the three Rs—Reduce, Reuse, Recycle—to make a difference.

The Aquarium has invited teens aged 14 to 18 from the Toronto area and beyond to join its Youth Advisory Council. This will give ecological stewards of the future some exciting opportunities to harness their passion for all things aquatic by lending expert advice on how to connect with other teens through conservation efforts and events.

5 TOP TIPS
for saving our oceans

1 CUT YOUR CARBON FOOTPRINT

You can help reduce the impact of climate change by finding ways to minimize your energy use.

2 CHOOSE YOUR SEAFOOD WISELY

Overfishing is causing devastating damage to the oceans. Choose seafood from populations that are both sustainable and healthy.

3 USE LESS PLASTIC

Much of our discarded plastic ends up in the ocean, where it kills marine animals, pollutes their habitat and litters our beaches.

4 LET THE SEA BE

Take nothing from the ocean you don't really need—that includes souvenirs or products such as sharkskin and coral—and don't put anything in it.

5 SUPPORT THE SCIENCE

Organizations that carry out research and conservation projects often rely on the financial support of individuals, and volunteers, to carry out their work.

Things to Do

Ripley's Aquarium of Canada offers an amazing range of experiences for visitors, either during our usual opening hours or at night, when you can sleep with the fishes.

Make new friends with horseshoe crabs in the Discovery Centre, rays in Ray Bay, and white spotted and brown banded sharks in the Shark Touch area. Educators are on hand to assure the safety of both children and animals and to answer any questions regarding these fascinating creatures.

Enjoy daily live dive shows at Ray Bay and Rainbow Reef. These feature a diver inside the habitat and an educator outside the habitat. Each show provides a great opportunity to learn more about the animals and their care. In Ray Bay, explore the world of sharks and stingrays while watching the rays feed out of our divers' hands. At the Rainbow Reef feeding show you can discover the world of coral reefs and the many colourful fish that call them home.

Curious to learn more about how the aquarists take care of all the animals in the Aquarium? Guided by one of our experienced educators on special tours, you can explore some of the behind-the-scenes animal husbandry areas and more.

Come to the Aquarium for an extraordinary overnight experience. Spend the evening exploring the galleries, participating in hands-on educational experiences, before tucking in to your sleeping bag and drifting off to sleep in the Dangerous Lagoon shark tunnel.

PUBLISHING

Publisher Anne Marshall
Editorial Director Rebecca Miles
Consultants Joe Choromanski, Andy Dehart
Researchers Charlotte Howell, James Proud, Dominic Lill
Art Director Sam South
Senior Designer Michelle Foster
Reprographics Juice Creative

For information regarding permission, write to
VP Intellectual Property
Ripley Entertainment, Inc.
Suite 188, 7576 Kingspointe Parkway
Orlando, Florida 32819, USA

Ripley's Aquarium of Canada
288 Bremner Boulevard
Toronto, Ontario M5V 3L9
(647) 351-FISH (3474)
www.ripleysaquariumofcanada.com

For information on visiting the Aquarium:
1. Download a QR barcode reader
   application for your smartphone
2. Open the app and point your camera
   phone at the graphic to learn more
   about the Aquarium.

MIX
Paper from
responsible sources
FSC® C011825
FSC
www.fsc.org

Printed in Canada on recycled papers using vegetable based inks.

PICTURE CREDITS

Cover Front: Mariusz S. Jurgielewicz - Shutterstock.com; Inside front and back: Andrew Williamson; Back: (t/r) Williyam Bradberry - Shutterstock.com, (t/c/l) Beth Swanson - Shutterstock.com, (c) Stephen Kerkhofs - Shutterstock.com

2 © iStock.com / dan_prat; 4 (throughout) file404 – Shutterstock.com, (throughout) vetryanaya_o – Shutterstock.com, (throughout) Gastev Roman – Shutterstock.com, (t/r) bluehand – Shutterstock.com, (tb/r) © NHPA/Photoshot, (t/c) Clay S. Turner – Shutterstock.com; 8 (b/r) Williyam Bradberry – Shutterstock.com; 9 (t/l) Beth Swanson – Shutterstock.com, (t/r) © NHPA/Photoshot, (b/r) Durden Images – Shutterstock.com; 10–11 Willyam Bradberry – Shutterstock.com; 12 (t/r) Eric Isselee – Shutterstock.com, (c/r) © NHPA/Photoshot; 15 (c/l) Joe B. Ruiz/ naturepl.com, (c/r) Photoshot; 16 Brandon Cole/ naturepl.com; 18 (c/l) Markus Gebauer – Shutterstock.com; 18–19 (b) Tischenko Irina – Shutterstock.com; 20 (t/r) © Georgette Douwma/naturepl.com; 20–21 (b) © Visuals Unlimited; 21 (t/r) © Bruce Coleman/Photoshot; 22–23 © Oceans-Image/Photoshot; 25 (t) Alex Mustard/ naturepl.com; 26–27 Andrew Williamson; 27 (t/r) Clay S. Turner – Shutterstock.com; 28 (c) Vilainecrevette – Shutterstock.com, (b) © NHPA/Photoshot; 29 (t/r) Brian Lasenby – Shutterstock.com; 30 Juan Garcia – Shutterstock.com; 31 (b/l) Peter Leahy – Shutterstock.com; 32–33 David Doubilet - National Geographic; 34 (t/r) (b/l) bluehand – Shutterstock.com; 35 (b/l) © NHPA/ Photoshot; 36 Andrew Burgess – Shutterstock.com; 37 (c/r) Beth Swanson – Shutterstock.com; 38 (b) TTL/Photoshot 39 Alex Mustard/naturepl.com; 40 Gerard Lacz/Rex Features; 41 (t/l) Photoshot, (t/r) Kristina Vackoca – Shutterstock.com, (b/r) © NHPA/Photoshot; 42–43 Rich Carey – Shutterstock.com; 44 (b) Durden Images – Shutterstock.com; 46–47 Stephen Kerkhofs – Shutterstock.com; 48 (c/r) Alex Mustard/naturepl.com, (b/l) Doug Perrine/naturepl.com; 50–51 Brian J. Skerry - National Geographic; 52–53 Marliusz S. Jurgielewicz – Shutterstock.com; 54 Ragma Images – Shutterstock.com; 55 (t/r) Kristina Vackova – Shutterstock.com, (b) NHPA/Photoshot; 58 (t/r) mangostock – Shutterstock.com; 58–59 James Wheeler – Shutterstock.com; 59 (t/l) Rob Marmion – Shutterstock.com, (c) Ethan Daniels – Shutterstock.com; 60 (t/r) Matt9122 – Shutterstock.com, (b/r) © iStock.com/svetikd; 61 fratisekhojdysz – Shutterstock.com; 62 (t/r) bluehand – Shutterstock.com

Key: t = top, b = bottom, c = center, l = left, r = right, sp = single page, dp = double page
All other photos are from Ripley Entertainment Inc.

Every attempt has been made to acknowledge correctly and contact copyright holders and we apologize in advance for any unintentional errors or omissions, which will be corrected in future editions.